# SHIPS OF SHADOWS: STORIES OF SHIPWRECKS

by Joy E. Dickerson

# TABLE OF CONTENTS

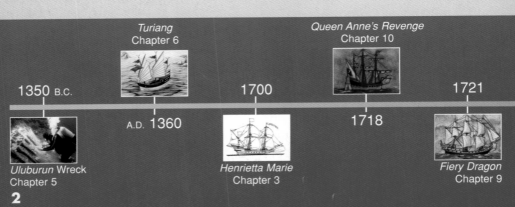

Turiang
Chapter 6

Queen Anne's Revenge
Chapter 10

1350 B.C.

A.D. 1360

1700

1718

1721

Uluburun Wreck
Chapter 5

Henrietta Marie
Chapter 3

Fiery Dragon
Chapter 9

# INTRODUCTION

## What Is a Ship?

What do you picture when you hear the word "ship"? Do you see a cruise ship with a swimming pool and guest cabins? Do you see a wooden ship with sails? Maybe you see an aircraft carrier with jets zooming off and landing.

Under the right conditions, even a gigantic aircraft carrier can sink.

These very different types of ships have one scary thing in common. They may all encounter storms, ice, enemy attacks, equipment failure, or human error. People have been sailing ships for thousands of years. And for all of that time, ships have been sinking.

This book tells the story of just a few of these notable shipwrecks.

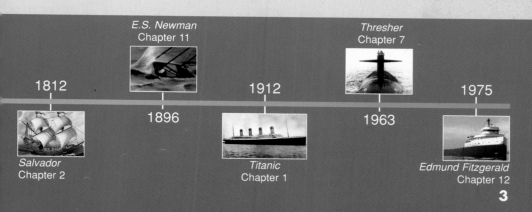

Salvador
Chapter 2

1812

E.S. Newman
Chapter 11

1896

Titanic
Chapter 1

1912

Thresher
Chapter 7

1963

1975

Edmund Fitzgerald
Chapter 12

# CHAPTER 1

## Ice Beneath the Waves

The ocean floor is cold and bare. It's an underwater desert. The sandy bottom is yellow in the light from the tiny submarine. Suddenly, a huge object appears. In the dim light, a rusty shape is revealed.

The wreck of the *Titanic* lies cold—but not forgotten—deep in the North Atlantic Ocean.

Close up, you see a railing. You see a deck. You see scattered dishes and luggage. A pair of shoes waits tidily for its owner. But no owner will ever return for those shoes. No one has needed those shoes since April 14, 1912. That's the day the *Titanic* sank.

Nearly 100 years ago, the *Titanic* set sail from Southampton, England. No on had ever seen a ship so big and so safe. The *Titanic*'s main job was to carry more than 2,000 passengers. It also carried general **cargo** from England to America.

The *Titanic* was as wide as a football field, and it was almost as long as nine football fields. Its **hull** had two layers of steel for extra strength. The hull was divided into separate airtight compartments. If one was punctured, the rest were supposed to keep the ship afloat.

The first—and last—voyage of the *Titanic* began on April 10. Signals flew back and forth from ship to shore. In the excitement, one message got overlooked. Icebergs had been seen in the *Titanic's* path. By the time the captain got this message, it was too late.

The *Titanic* before her trip to New York

The white tip of an iceberg loomed up in front of the ship. More of the iceberg was under the water. The ship could not turn in time. The iceberg punctured six of the airtight compartments on the ship. In less than three hours, the ship sank. There were not enough lifeboats on the ship. Only 707 of the 2,220 passengers were rescued. The others hold their secrets deep in the icy waters in which they drowned.

# CHAPTER 2

## Storm in the Bay

In the spring of 1812, the ship *Salvador* sailed from Spain to Montevideo, the largest city in Uruguay. The people of Uruguay did not want Spain to rule them anymore. The *Salvador*'s mission was to keep Spain in control.

On August 12, the ship approached Uruguay's coast. The 500 soldiers onboard were eager to do their job, but the weather didn't cooperate. As the ship sailed into the mouth of the Rio de la Plata, the wind rose, and a storm engulfed it.

The wind came from the southwest. The captain of the *Salvador* didn't know that this meant danger when he sailed into the shallow waters of Maldonado Bay. He thought the ship would be safe there, but the ship was too deep for the bay.

The *Salvador* sank in the shallow waters of Maldonado Bay, near Montevideo, Uruguay.

The *Salvador* got stuck on a **sandbar**. The winds drove it over on its side. The heavy cannons came loose and slid across the decks, killing many soldiers. Others were killed when the heavy, wet canvas sails fell down and smothered them.

A few sailors tried to swim to safety. But most of the men onboard didn't know how to swim. They drowned when the ship sank. By the morning of August 13, 1812, nearly 400 people had died.

The people of Uruguay celebrated when they heard the grim news. The sinking of the *Salvador* meant that Spain would no longer control them. When the cannons were raised from the wreck in 1998, the people of Uruguay saw them as symbols of victory.

The *Salvador*'s wooden sides decayed long ago. Here a diver is working to release one of the four bronze cannons found on the site.

# CHAPTER 3

## Manacles Off Key West

On the sandy bottom of the Caribbean lie chains. They never helped lift an anchor or hold a gate. Instead, the chains were attached to metal cuffs called *manacles*. The manacles kept African people prisoner in the hold of the *Henrietta Marie*.

For 150 years, people were sold into slavery from Africa. The

Journalist Michael H. Cottman (on right), a member of the National Association of Black Scuba Divers, helps place a marker on the site where the *Henrietta Marie* sank.

*Henrietta Marie* sailed early in the slave trade. In 1700, it took its last journey. The captain bought slaves in West Africa. He loaded them into his ship like they were cargo. He chained them to the inner hull of the ship with manacles.

On the journey across the Atlantic, about a third of these people died. The captain sold his human cargo in Jamaica a few months later.

As the *Henrietta Marie* made its way north from Jamaica, a storm hit. Just off the island of Key West, Florida, high waves swamped the ship, and it sank. All the crew was lost. Were the Africans lucky to escape the sinking of the *Henrietta Marie*? It isn't much of a choice—to go down with the ship or to live as a slave. But at least the **descendants** of those survivors had a chance to experience freedom.

Over the next 272 years, the wooden ship gradually decayed. At last, all that remained were the most vivid symbols of the ship's work—the manacles. The wreckage was discovered in 1972.

The *Henrietta Marie* is the only known wreckage of a slave ship to be found in American waters. It bears witness to the sad story of slavery in the Americas.

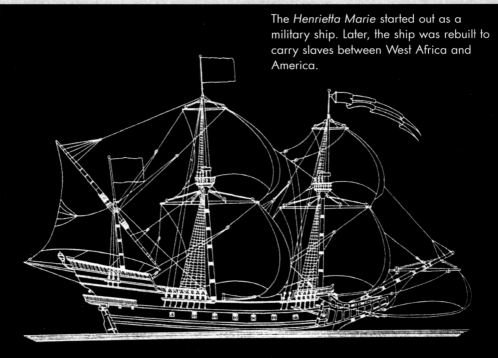

The *Henrietta Marie* started out as a military ship. Later, the ship was rebuilt to carry slaves between West Africa and America.

# CHAPTER 4

## Echoes and Images

Side-scanning sonar is used on the ocean floor. The brightest part of this radar screen pictured here shows the location of a shipwreck.

People have looked for shipwrecks for as long as ships have been wrecking! It was important to recover a ship's cargo. Until the 1940s, only ships in very shallow water could be **salvaged** easily. In 1943, **scuba** equipment was invented.

Scuba divers could stay underwater for up to an hour. With weights on their belts, they could go deeper than ever before. The *Salvador* and the *Henrietta Marie* were discovered by scuba divers in shallow water. The *Titanic*, however, was in much deeper water.

There is no light in deep water, and it is very cold. The pressure of the water there can crush a person. Only recently has equipment been invented that makes discovery of deeper wrecks possible. Two types of equipment are used to explore deep-sea shipwrecks.

Side-scan sonar makes maps of the ocean floor. The side-scan sonar sends sounds over a wide path. The sounds bounce off the floor and find anything that is on it. Then, submersibles are sent down for a closer look. The wreck of the *Edmund Fitzgerald* was found with side-scan sonar.

Submersibles are tiny submarines. Sometimes they can hold one or two people. Often, though, they are operated by remote control from a ship on the surface. They are called "remote operated vehicles," or ROVs.

ROVs took pictures of the *Titanic* and even collected objects and brought them to the surface. Some people want to bring up all the objects on shipwrecks. Other people think the shipwrecks should be left alone and viewed as honored historical places. What do you think?

This ROV acts as the eyes and hands of researchers. It is equipped with lights, cameras, and robot arms that can pick up objects and carry them to the surface.

# CHAPTER 5

## Ingots in the Mediterranean

On an afternoon in 1982, a diver's head broke the surface of the water. The diver was excited. About 170 feet below, he had been hunting for sponges. Instead, he found bars of metal—ingots.

TURKEY

GREEK ISLES

The diver had found what scientists believe is the oldest shipwreck yet discovered. The ship probably sank around 1350 B.C.

A diver on the wreck of the *Uluburun*

The wreck lay in the Mediterranean Sea, just off the coast of Turkey near the town of Uluburun (oo•loo•**boo**•roon). We don't know the actual name of the ship, so it is named for the nearest town.

The diver told archaeologists about the wreck. Archaeologists are scientists who study ancient things. Divers uncovered gold jewelry on the wreck. But to the scientists, other items in the wreck were more important.

The jars on the ship helped scientists figure out the ship's age. The jars are called *amphorae* (**am**•fuh•ree). Amphorae are rounded on the bottom and have narrow necks with "ears." The ears are rounded handles.

The style of the jars lets archaeologists know when and where they were made. From this information, the archaeologists could tell when the ship was sailing and where it could have gone on its voyage.

Scientists think the *Uluburun* was a royal ship. That would explain the wealth of metals and jewelry. Ten ingots of copper were found for every one ingot of tin on the ship. That is exactly the amount needed to make bronze—the metal that defined the Bronze Age.

Amphorae are found in ancient shipwrecks in the Mediterranean. They were used to ship grains and liquids. They were the packing crates of their day.

Copper and tin ingots weren't the only metals found on *Uluburun*. Gold jewelry was also found.

# CHAPTER 6

## Monsoon in Malaysia

The ship struggled to steer into the wind. Gigantic waves rising high over the *Turiang* made it look like a toy. Howling winds whipped the sails, making pennants and flags snap.

The *Turiang*'s paint was fresh. It was a new ship—strong and sturdy. In its hold, it carried box after box of beautiful dishes. These dishes helped make the *Turiang* stable in the turbulent seas.

But youth and strength were not enough for the *Turiang*. The **monsoon** winds off the coast of Malaysia were too wild. The towering waves were too high. Soon water washed over the sides, causing the ship to founder and sink.

This is what the *Turiang* probably looked like. The artist based this drawing on ships from the same time period that carried similar cargoes.

The *Turiang* was a trading ship in Southeast Asia. It picked up dishes, iron, and other goods at some ports and sold them at other ports. It visited ports in China, Thailand, Vietnam, Malaysia, Java, and Borneo. Many trading ships sailed in this area.

The wreck of the *Turiang* was discovered in the 1990s. Fishing nets had torn off the top decks, but much of the cargo was still there. Cartons of dishes were in perfect condition. By examining how the ship was built, scientists dated it to the middle 1300s. Rusty nail holes identified the ship as Chinese. No one else built with iron nails at that time. The ship lacked "**sacrificial** planks." Sacrificial planks were pieces of wood nailed each year to the hull of ships to keep shipworms from eating the wood of the ship. Because the *Turiang* didn't have sacrificial planks, scientists could tell that it had only sailed on a few voyages.

The *Turiang*'s cargo is reaching buyers at last. But no one is eating off of these plates! They are price-less collectors' items.

# CHAPTER 7

## Implosion Near Nantucket

The submarine *Thresher* glided through the water. At 1,300 feet below the ocean's surface, it ran deeper than any submarine had run before. The *Thresher* had a state-of-the-art **nuclear engine**. It was a model of what a submarine could do.

On April 10, 1963, at about 9:00 A.M., something went wrong. For some reason, the engine shut itself down. Working furiously, the crew tried to blow out the water they carried to make the sub heavy. If they could clear the water tanks, they would rise rapidly.

No luck—the tanks would not empty. The controls would not operate properly at that depth. At 9:12 A.M., the *Thresher* **radioed** to the surface. "Experiencing minor difficulties…Am attempting to blow…Will keep you informed."

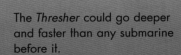
The *Thresher* could go deeper and faster than any submarine before it.

Just a few minutes later, the *Thresher* was gone. The crew didn't have the time it needed to restart the engine. The weight of 1,300 feet of water caused an **implosion** that crushed the submarine. All 129 people aboard died at that moment.

By investigating the wreck, the Navy learned many things about operating deep beneath the ocean. They made changes in submarines and in the procedures sailors followed. In that sense, the crew of the *Thresher* did not die in vain.

The Navy had to develop new equipment to explore the wreck of the *Thresher*. They had never tried to work that deep beneath the ocean. Much of the equipment used today to explore shipwrecks was developed to investigate the sunken *Thresher*.

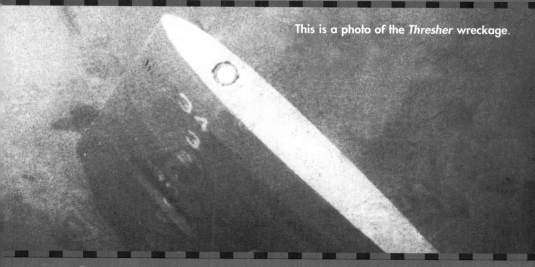

This is a photo of the *Thresher* wreckage.

# CHAPTER 8

## Labs and Libraries

"People ask me what's the most fabulous discovery I've ever made," George Bass says. "And I always say it's been in the library. The big discoveries are always in the library, or in the **conservation** labs."

George Bass is called the father of underwater archaeology. He directed the work at the *Uluburun* wreck site. For him, it's fun to dive and dig. But the real work is done elsewhere.

In the library, researchers look at old records. The British Library holds the records of thousands of ship journeys. The records tell when ships sailed and what they carried. When divers find a ship in a certain place with a certain cargo, they may find a match at the British Library.

Scientists also use the library to find out about objects. A book on ancient pottery might help set a date for a newly discovered shipwreck. Records of how ships were built helped identify the *Turiang* as a Chinese ship.

Objects from shipwrecks lie in seawater for centuries. When brought to the surface, they can decay quickly. Special techniques **stabilize** the objects to keep them from decaying.

This cannon raised from the *Queen Anne's Revenge* was soaked in water for more than two years to stabilize it.

Objects undergo months of treatment in laboratories to stabilize them. They are cleaned and preserved. They are studied and measured. Sometimes they are encased in plastic for protection. Only then may the objects be handled, displayed, or sold.

# CHAPTER 9

## Treasure Off Madagascar

Billy One-Hand, also known as Christopher Condent, took one last look back. As he watched, the **bow** of his former ship sank beneath the waves. It had been a good ship. He and his crew had captured riches beyond any pirate's dream.

**Pirates** were the highway robbers of the seas. For years pirates attacked ships in the Caribbean and Atlantic oceans.

This flag flew over Christopher Condent's ship.

Now, on January 16, 1721, Captain One-Hand was saying good-bye to the pirate life. The French government offered all pirates amnesty. Amnesty meant they would no longer be outlaws, but they had to give up being pirates. They had to sink the *Fiery Dragon*.

Captain One-Hand and his crew were rich. Every one of the 300 pirates was a millionaire. One-Hand was so well liked and trusted that he was elected to be captain of the *Fiery Dragon*.

The wreck of the *Fiery Dragon* was found in the late 1990s. The divers were looking for the ship of Captain Kidd, another famous pirate. They found One-Hand's ship instead. The objects the divers found confirmed its identity.

Captain Billy One-Hand commanded the *Fiery Dragon*. After he sank the *Fiery Dragon*, he lived peacefully in France.

The *Fiery Dragon* attacked ships on both sides of the Atlantic. One of its famous captures was a ship called the *House of Austria*. Divers on the *Fiery Dragon* found dishes that were clearly from the *House of Austria*.

Another famous capture was an Arabian ship sailing to India. The cargo taken would be worth $375 million today. The pirates took gold, diamonds, other jewels, and silk. Each pirate took a share of the wealth before they sank the *Fiery Dragon*.

# CHAPTER 10

## Cannons at Beaufort Inlet

On a hot, sunny day in June 1718, a wooden ship sailed between two small islands that guarded the coast of North Carolina. The islands also hid a bay called Beaufort Inlet. The ship was loaded with treasure, so it needed a place to hide.

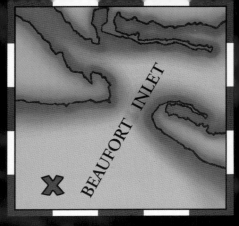

The *Queen Anne's Revenge* was the ship of Blackbeard the Pirate.

The ship was called the *Queen Anne's Revenge*. For over a year—since 1717— its captain had been Edmund Teach, better known as Blackbeard the Pirate. From the Virgin Islands north to Charleston, Blackbeard created terror.

Now, the *Queen Anne's Revenge* was full. The stolen coins, jewels, and other goods made the ship ride low in the water. It was time to drop anchor in the inlet and split up the treasure. Each of the over 300 sailors would

Suddenly, the ship shuddered. A scraping sound could only mean one thing. The heavy ship was stuck on a sandbar. The sailors groaned. It would be hard work to free the ship. But Blackbeard looked thoughtful.

He ordered most of the treasure moved to another ship in his fleet. He and a few sailors moved to that ship and sailed off! He left 25 of his sailors stranded on the sandbar. Now the treasure would be divided among fewer sailors. As he sailed away, he could see the *Queen Anne's Revenge* begin to tip over.

The sailors left behind screamed and cursed. As they watched, the *Queen Anne's Revenge* sank under the water. The stranded sailors were later rescued by another pirate ship, but they never caught up with Blackbeard.

They were the last people to see the *Queen Anne's Revenge* for the next 300 years. In the 1990s, the wreck of the ship was found, and many objects (but no treasure) were salvaged.

Nearly 300 years after the *Queen Anne's Revenge* sank, her cannons were salvaged by North Carolina's Underwater Archaeology Unit.

# CHAPTER 11

## Rescue at Pea Island

Winds howled, forcing the three-masted schooner against the rocky shore on October 11, 1896. Driving rain poured from a **roiling** sky. The signal flare

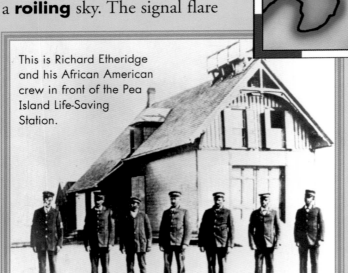

This is Richard Etheridge and his African American crew in front of the Pea Island Life-Saving Station.

NORTH CAROLINA

PEA ISLAND

X

glowed and then fizzled out. Huge waves broke over the beach like giant claws, dragging whatever they touched back into the sea.

The elements were competing. Which would defeat the rescue of the *E.S. Newman*'s crew? On the shore, the rescue crew from Station 17 on Pea Island struggled to reach the ship.

The rain soaked their gunpowder. That meant the rescuers could not shoot a rescue line to the ship with their line-throwing gun. Their small, flat-bottomed surfboat would be torn apart in the angry waves.

But this was one of the best rescue crews in the U.S. Life-Saving Service. Their leader, Richard Etheridge, made quick decisions. He called for the two best swimmers on his six-person crew. If one swimmer couldn't reach the ship, maybe two swimmers could.

He tied the two swimmers together and gave them an extra line. He sent them out in the churning sea. They waded. They swam. They crawled. Finally, they reached the *E.S. Newman*. They grabbed the first sailor from the ship and hauled him to shore.

Nine times in six hours, two rescuers went out to the ship. And nine times in six hours, three people returned to shore. From shore, they watched as the ship, the *E.S. Newman,* was pounded into pieces. The ship was lost, but all hands were saved.

The *E.S. Newman* was blown against the rocky outer banks of North Carolina near Pea Island. This stretch of coast is so dangerous that it is called "the Graveyard of the Atlantic."

# CHAPTER 12

## Lost on the Lake

LAKE SUPERIOR

X

"We are holding our own," the captain of the *Edmund Fitzgerald* radioed to a nearby ship. These were the last words ever heard from the ship. A fierce storm raged across Lake Superior. Storms like this were sent by "the witch of November," according to sailors.

On November 10, 1975, the *Edmund Fitzgerald* carried a full load of more than 26,000 tons of iron ore. It was one of the biggest, fastest ships ever to travel the waters of the Great Lakes. Like the *Titanic,* the *Edmund Fitzgerald* was considered to be unsinkable.

Now, huge waves rose over the ship—giant walls of water. Winds tried to push the *Edmund Fitzgerald* over onto its side. The radar that guided it went out. The *Fitzgerald* radioed, "I have sustained some… damage." The *Fitzgerald* was taking on water.

The *Edmund Fitzgerald* was called "The Pride of the American Side."

A nearby ship agreed to help the *Fitzgerald* get to Whitefish Bay, which was sheltered from storms. Slowly, the ships limped onward. At 7:10 P.M., the captain's last words were heard. A few minutes later, the *Edmund Fitzgerald* disappeared from radar.

Was the *Fitzgerald* driven to the bottom of the lake by a mighty wave? Did its hull rip open as it hit the lake bottom in the **trough** of a wave? Did the wind cause damage that allowed water into the hold? No one survived to tell the story. All hands were lost. The ship now lies on the bottom of Lake Superior, broken into two pieces. Its bow sits upright. Its stern rests upside down. The center part of the ship has been crushed.

Every year on November 10, a bell rings out over the churning waters of Lake Superior. The bell rings 29 times. The bell was brought up from the wreck of the *Edmund Fitzgerald*. It rings once for each of the sailors who lost his life when the ship went down.

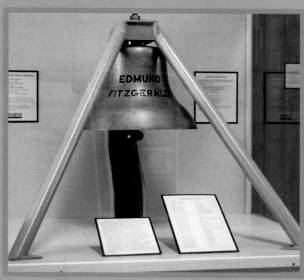

This is the bell from the *Edmund Fitzgerald*.

# APPENDIX

## Parts of a Ship

The most basic parts of a ship stay the same no matter how big, small, ancient, or modern the ship is! A modern ship may have a steam engine instead of sails. It may have smokestacks instead of masts. But it still has *fore* and *aft*, *starboard* and *port*, *hull* and *hold*.

**Port**—the left side of a ship when facing forward

**Stern**—the rear end of a ship

**Steering wheel**—the wheel that operates the rudder, turning the ship

**Rudder**—the steering mechanism of a ship, operated by the wheel

**Keel**—the very bottom of a ship

**Aft**—toward the stern; after

**Starboard**—the right side of a ship when facing forward

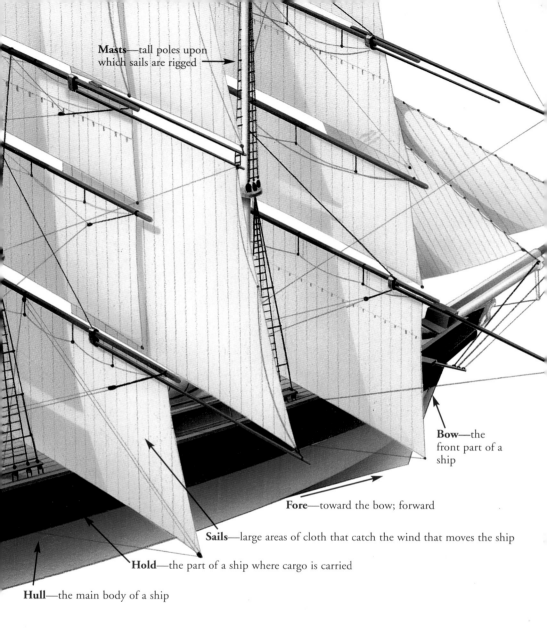

**Masts**—tall poles upon which sails are rigged

**Bow**—the front part of a ship

**Fore**—toward the bow; forward

**Sails**—large areas of cloth that catch the wind that moves the ship

**Hold**—the part of a ship where cargo is carried

**Hull**—the main body of a ship

**29**

# GLOSSARY

**bow**      (bow) the front end of a ship

**cargo**      (**kar**•goh) the goods a ship carries

**conservation**      (kon•sur•**vay**•shuhn) protection from further damage

**descendant**      (di•**sen**•duhnt) a grandchild, great-grandchild, and so on

**hull**      (hul) the body of a ship or boat

**implosion**      (im•**ploh**•zhuhn) a violent collapse inward

**monsoon**      (mon•**soon**) a huge, seasonal storm in Southeast Asia

**nuclear engine**      (**noo**•klee•uhr **en**•jin) an engine that gets power from a nuclear reaction

**pirate**      (**py**•rit) an oceangoing outlaw who attacked and stole from other ships

**radio**      (**ray**•dee•oh) to communicate by radio

**roiling**      (**royl**•ing) churning and boiling

**sacrificial**   (sak•ruh•**fish**•uhl) to be given up or sacrificed

**salvage**   (**sal**•vij) to save from loss or destruction

**sandbar**   (**sand**•bar) a sandy, raised area of the sea floor, often temporary

**scuba**   (**skoo**•buh) self-contained underwater breathing apparatus; air tanks that let divers stay underwater for an extended period of time

**stabilize**   (**stay**•buh•lyz) to keep from decay; to make stable

**trough**   (trawf) the lowest point of a wave

# INDEX